The Who, What, Where, Why and How Principles of

Developing CRE

Printed in the United States of America, Published by Wehr Publishing dba for Otali Solutions, LLC

Copyright © 2016 by Wehr Ventures, dba for Otali Solutions LLC, All Rights Reserved

ISBN:-13:978-0984534623

ISBN:-10:0984534628

LCCN:-2015956159

The Who, What, Where, Why and How Principles of
Developing CRE

WehrVentures

ABOUT THE AUTHOR:

Mr. Wehrmeyer is a Texas lawyer, commercial real estate developer, and professor at the University of Texas-San Antonio, teaching real estate development and finance. Bob has experience developing commercial real and purchasing/selling of land. Bob has published numerous articles and books including; *"The Complete Guide to Developing Commercial Real Estate, the Who, What, Where, Why and How Principles of Developing Commercial Real Estate"* (updated and reprinted 2013) and the book, *"How to Develop Commercial Real Estate, Part I"* (2014).

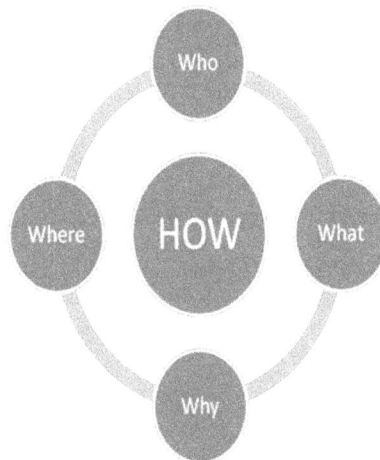

CONTENTS:

HOW TO USE THIS GUIDE:

This Guide and the deliverables outlined should be completed in conjunction with reading the authors book, *"The Complete Guide to Developing Commercial Real Estate, The Who, What, Where, Why and How Principles of Developing Commercial Real Estate* ("Principles Book") and/or watching or listening to the authors Video Series discussing the principles of the book. In this regard you will find numerous areas in this Guide that refer the reader to the relevant chapter of the Principles Book for further information.

In order to help facilitate the deliverable exercise and process we have made certain assumptions. These assumptions are outlined and marked throughout the Guide as, "ASSUME" and available at the end of the Guide for review. If you have more specific information related to a project use the actual information rather than the assumptions.

This Guide references numerous Attachments. The Attachments are meant as reference sources only and should not be copied or modified as part of the deliverable process. Many of the Attachments are products from prior students that have taken the authors course. The reader can access and view additional samples of the Attachments as well as purchase the Principles Book and the Video Series by visiting the company website at www.developingcre.com or www.wehrventures.com.

ABOUT THIS GUIDE: THE DEVELOPMENT SUMMARY

The following workbook or Guide outlines many but not all of the material steps involved in developing commercial real estate. Some areas are emphasized more that others to help simplify the process. The Guide is broken into the major steps in the process, a few tips or insights marked with a blue arrow, definitions of important terms and introduction of the key professionals. The approach to development outlined in this Guide assumes a commercial merchant type development effort. A merchant development effort is one where the developer will utilize traditional commercial financing and attempt to sell the finished project as soon as it is stabilized.

If you are participating in the deliverable exercise outlined in this Guide the responses should be downloaded to a development summary. The format and presentation for the summery is up to you-the developer. There are samples of project development summaries and final development plans available on the company web site at www.developingcre.com or www.wehrventures.com.

The Who, What, Where, Why and How Principles of

Developing CRE

TIP #1: FOUR BASIC PHASES FOR COMMERCIAL DEVELOPMENT

1. Vision/Pre-Development
2. Construction
3. Management/Operations
4. Refinancing or Sale

There are four basic phases in almost every commercial real estate development; vision/pre-development, construction, management/operations and refinancing or sale. As the developer of commercial real estate you will spend most of your time in the vision, pre-development phase of the project. In the vision/pre-development phase you must ask and answer all the key questions that are necessary to determine if a project is feasible. This book will present the vision/pre-development phase in five (5) parts. The five (5) parts will outline what key questions to ask and answer as set forth in the Principles book, and Video Series, "The Complete Guide to Developing Commercial Real Estate, The Who, What, Where, Why and How Principles to Developing Commercial Real Estate".

The Who, What, Where, Why and How Principles of
Developing CRE

PART 1: THE VISION:

What are You Going to Build,
Where are You Going to Build it, and
Who are You Building it For?

1

TIP #2: The "RULE OF COMPS" – COMPARABLE PROJECTS

Throughout this Guide we will refer to, "the Rule of Comps". Utilizing the Rule of Comps can help you determine almost every aspect of the initial vision and project specifics. Comparable (or comps) in a real estate sense means similar; similar in type, size, location, quality and features. For example in order to determine a fair price for land you will want to know the actual sales price of similar surrounding land parcels or even the asking price of similar land parcels currently for sale. If you want to know what tenants you might be able to attract to the project study the tenant mix of existing comparable and surrounding projects. By studying comparable development projects you can determine almost every aspect of what might make sense for your development from what rent they are charging to other items like; building size and layout, architectural design features, benefits and amenities, average rent and lease terms and even how long it took to fill up the building with tenants. You can gather most of this information by researching the internet. However visiting with local commercial real estate broker, building owners, bankers and, other developers is also very helpful.

The Rule of Comps can be applied to help almost every aspect of a commercial real estate development project. When in doubt base initial project decision on comparable project information-follow the Rule of Comps!

KEY PROFESSIONALS: THE CIVIL ENGINEER

In the early stages of the development process the "civil" can help the developer understand the many complex land and use issues involved in a commercial real estate development effort. Many civil engineers will also work with the developer on initial land plan concepts like helping the developer place the building footprints on the development site. In the early development of the project you can rely on the civil to work with platting, (street, drains, water, sewer, roads and others) and, permitting (architectural, civil, structural, mechanical, electrical, plumbing, landscape, irrigation, fire safety and others).

In addition to the above the civil can be engaged to prepare or oversee; storm water management plan, water pollution abatement plan, sanitary sewer plan, flood studies, all utility related issues including the utility service agreement, tree preservation plans, endangered species assessment, traffic impact analysis, archaeology and historical studies and other specific issues related to the land and the intended use.

STEP 1: The Vision and What do You Want to Build?

The vision for a commercial real estate project often starts with knowing what product you want to build. This is typically either driven by a tenant relationship the developer has or an expertize the developer has acquired through experience. For purposes of this exercise if you don't already have a vision for what you want to develop choose one of the following:

- *Retail*
- *Office*
- *Industrial*
- *Multi-Family*

(i.e., apartments, townhomes, senior-living)

- *Specialty: Hotel, Self-Storage, Other*

STEP 2: The Vision: Refine the Vision

To help simplify and narrow all the choices in the initial stages of the development process this Guide will outline or focus on the basic steps for either a commercial office or retail project. With this in mind, If you decide to develop an office for the development project try to refine the office development by choosing one of the following office product types:

- *Class A*

- *Class B*

- *Class C*

Class A

Buildings competing for premier office/retail users with rents above average. Buildings have high quality finishes, high quality "MEP" systems, exceptional accessibility, quality benefits, features and compelling location.

Class B

Buildings competing for a wide range of users with rents in the average range for the area. Building finishes are acceptable for the location and systems are standard, but the building traditionally does not compete with Class A at the same price unless location is compelling.

Class C

Often second generation space and buildings, typically older and competing for tenants who are looking for basic functions and systems with rents at or below the average for the area.

STEP 2 (cont'd.): Product Type; Office or Retail?

If you prefer to develop a retail project for the development refine the vision by choosing one of the following retail: types:

- **Corner Store**

  These centers typically rare less than 5,000 square feet may have one or two tenants beside the corner

  store and found on neighborhood streets or corners typically catering to the impulse buyer.

- **Convenience Center**

  These centers typically range between 5,000 and 25,000 square feet with services designed for local needs

  and surrounding neighborhoods.

- **Neighborhood Center**

  Neighborhood centers can range anywhere from 50,000 - 100,000 square feet and usually anchored with

  a basic services provider like grocery store with supporting shadow tenants that complement the anchor tenant.

- **Community Center**

  Community centers are typically from 100,000-300,000 squares feet with 20-70 leasable spaces ranging

  from lease anchor to restaurants to retailers.

- **Regional and Power Centers**

  Typically ranging from 500,000-1,000,000 or more square footage, Lease mixed use centers, numerous anchors, shadows and other.

STEP 3: The Vision Phase and Identifying Comparable Projects

In Step 3 attempt to identify no less than three existing commercial real estate projects comparable to the one you want to build. The comps should be similar not only to what you envision the project or building to look like but if possible the location and demographics should be similar. As you refine your vision the comps may change. That's okay but remember almost everything about the comparable projects will be important to you in determining how you might model your own project. Comp information is an important feature in any development plan so add a summary of the selected comps to the development summary.

NOTE: Most new office/retail development projects will have a web site. From this website you can get a lot of information about the comps-especially information important to attracting rent paying tenants. The comps will be helpful not only in formulating the initial vision but in determining almost every aspect of the project development. Items like typical market lease rates, TI allowances, NNN costs and typical length of lease as well as projected "lease up" time and even site and floor plan design.

STEP 4: The Vision and Estimating Project Type and Size

A new CRE development project is typically driven by one or more of the following: developer tenant relationship, developer project expertise or a great location. Assuming you do not already have a site in mind or targeted tenant the project vision can help you determine the kind of site you might need. As mentioned in Step 3 comps or competitive projects can help you determine many issues related to your vision and project. For Step 4 however you need begin refining project size and type.

For example: the developer's initial thoughts for a new office development might be a rectangular shaped 30,000 square foot, two story office building. Each floor in the early vision for the project might have @15,000 square feet to rent.

With this level of an initial vision you can look for a land site that is suitable in size and characteristic for the project. If you already have a land site in mind you can design the project considering both the project vision and the site characteristics. Of course don't forget who you are building the project for-the tenant. Attracting rent paying tenants is the most important aspect of any commercial real estate development. The project broker or civil engineer can be very helpful in addressing appropriate type and size of the project.

Definitions: Gross Square Footage:

Office buildings, retail centers and other commercial real estate projects have exterior walls, elevator shafts and stairwells typically not considered "leasable" or "rentable" space. Therefore, if you are thinking 30,000 in rentable square footage for the project you will need to increase the overall building size. The contractor will quote you a construction price based on Gross Square Footage ("GSF") not rentable square footage ("RSF"). GSF measures the building from exterior wall to exterior wall. With this in mind, ASSUME you need to increase original building footprint concept by 10-15%. In our example from Step 3; 30,000(.15) =3,450. For a total gross square footage (GSF) of 33,450 square feet or rounded up to 33,500 GSF.

NOTE: The 15 percent additional square footage is an estimate only. Retail buildings for example might be 5-10 percent increase in GSF while a single user building might require very little increase or add-on to GSF. Discuss this issue with a civil engineer or general contractor.

STEP 5: The Vision and Selecting a Location

A project vision often starts with a piece of land; location location, location. The golden rule of real estate. Location is important for many reasons but from a developers perspective location attracts tenants and users to the intended development. Tenants pay rent and rent attracts financing (more about that later) However the land parcel must not only attract tenants it must be appropriate for the intended project vision. Therefore it must be large enough to accommodate not only the estimated building footprint but parking, sidewalks, lighting, detention, internal roadways, land-scaping, offsets and other important needs and functions. The project civil engineer, architect and even broker can help estimate the lot size needed.

For purposes of this Guide for a one or two story building in a suburban area you can ASSUME no less than one acre for every 10,000-15,000 square feet of building. With these issues and the project vision in mind for Step 5 choose a site location. Once a site is chosen download information on the chosen location to the development summary. NOTE: If you are participating in the development process it is wise to find a building site that is listed with a commercial broker. If the chosen site is in an "urban" area as opposed to "suburban", area you will need to discuss appropriate lot and project size with a civil engineer, architect or broker.

SEE ATTACHMENT A FOR LOCATION MAPS SAMPLES.

KEY PROFESSIONALS: THE ARCHITECT AND DESIGN TEAM

The architect and design team will be the group that takes your vision and translates this vision into something that can be read, understood and built. The most common approach to commercial construction today is the "designs, bid, build" process. The design, bid, build approach assumes the architect designs the project based on the developer vision. The architect then embodies the building in a series of drawings referred to as "plans and specs". The architect and the developer can then use these drawings or plans and specs to bid out the project construction requirement. Once the project is "bid out" a general contractor is selected to build the project.

Early in the development of a project the developer needs the architect and design team to help with numerous issues including but not limited to the following: renderings, elevations, site plans, models, floor plans and coordination with the various engineers and contractor. The architect is also typically part of the on-going construction review. At the delivery of the finished project the architect should sign off on the construction work as completed in substantial compliance with the plans and specs (subject only to a final punch list).

Go to AIA.org and review or download a standard AIA service agreement between the owner and the Architect. Most bank lenders and equity investors will expect a contract between the you and the project architect.

STEP 6: The Vision and Creating Initial Site Plan

Once you have identified a potential site and have a initial vision of what you want to build you can begin to think about how the buildings and other features might appear on the site. One easy way to start this process is to outline how you believe people will get into and out of the site. Access to and from the site along with internal roadways can help you understand how to position the buildings on the site.

For Step 6 attempt to create an initial site plan. For purposes of this Guide the initial site plan can be hand drawn. There are numerous sites on the internet that can help you create a site plan using the actual development location. Don't forget about the comps as a good source for how the buildings and other features might appear on the site. When designing a site plan try to keep in mind the natural landscape. When possible avoid removing large trees and attempt to incorporate or design around existing streams, hillsides and other natural conditions.

SEE ATTACHMENT B FOR SAMPLES OF SITE PLANS.

STEP 7: The Vision and Creating a Picture, Drawing or Rendering

Early in the development process you need to determine not only how the buildings and other features might fit on the land site but also how you want the buildings to look. The easiest way to do this without paying an architect or designer to create a rendering is to study the comps and research the internet for ideas and examples. Studying the comps identified in Step 3 can help give you an initial idea of how you want your project to look. For STEP 7 you must conduct Internet research, tour the surrounding area and/or meet with draftsman or architect to create an initial impression for how you want the buildings to look.

SEE ATTACHMENT C FOR SAMPLES OF VARIOUS PICTURES, DRAWINGS OR RENDERINGS.

STEP 8: The Vision and Attracting Tenants and Users

For Step 8 focus in on who you want to attract as the project tenants and users. Almost everyone involved in the development process wants to understand the target market and demographics of the community and area surrounding the development project. For STEP 8 research the internet or work with a real estate broker and determine the key market information, surrounding tenant mix and demographics for the location. Focus on the information the targeted tenants and users will find important in making a leasing decision.

Typically the demographic information should include a study of the surrounding area conveying information important to the intended tenants. This should include population numbers by age group, education levels and income data. The demographic report should encompass, no less than a 1/3/5 mile surrounding the project location. Summarize the data important to the project and add to development summary. NOTE: if the site was listed with a commercial real estate broker chances are much of this data including surrounding tenant information is already available.

SEE THE WHERE SECTION OF THE PRINCIPLES BOOK.

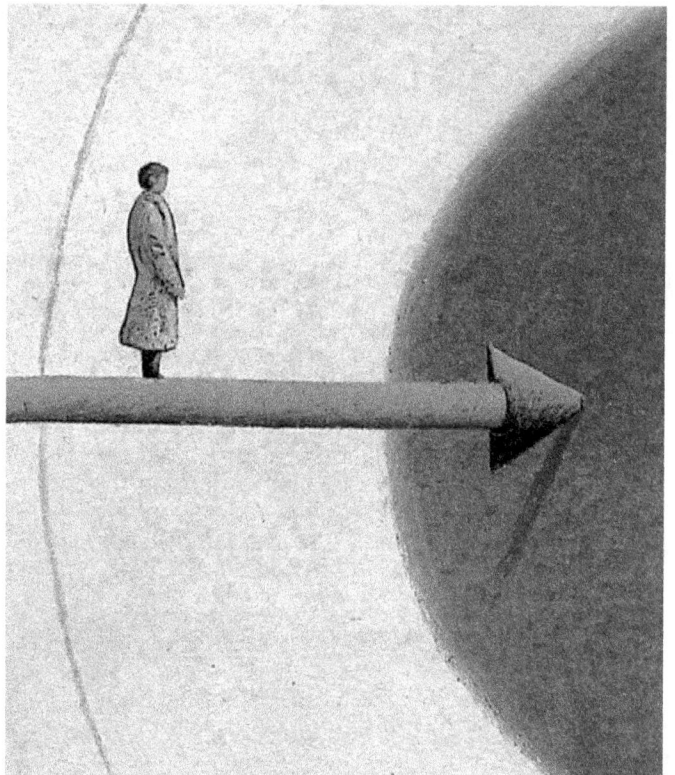

TIP #3: "Build it and the Tenants will Come", Product Types

In the movie, "Field of Dreams", the great actor, James Earl Jones states, "build it and they will come, they will definitely come". Even though Mr. Jones is referring to a soon to be built baseball field in the movie it personifies the reality of developer risk. Many commercial real estate projects alleviate some of the developer risk by "pre-leasing". Pre-leasing means rent paying tenants commit to a lease agreement before the developer invests a lot of money in a project. Office and retail projects are examples of development projects where tenants sign leases before the project is built. In fact, many construction lenders and equity investors expect these types of projects to be significantly pre-leased before the loan closes or equity is invested.

However, some commercial project types do not traditionally pre-lease. Apartment projects, are good examples of this type of commercial real estate development. The author refers to these types as, "build it and the tenants will come" development projects. This Guide focuses on product type that require pre-leasing because the tenant leasing process is important part in the overall responsibility of the developer. If you are thinking of developing a project type that does not require pre-leasing; apartment, self-storage and hotels being a few of these product types you will need to spend a lot of time focused on the steps related to market demand, demographics and project related comparable's. More importantly, focus on the issues important to the tenants you want to attract to your project.

PART 2: THE DEVELOPMENT PHASE
What are the Specific Issues with the
Intended Use, Site and Targeted Tenants

TIP #4: "Feasibility Period, Diligence and the "BIG SIX"

Once you have determined an initial vision for the project and selected a land site you begin to transition from the vision phase to project pre-development phase. The pre-development phase consists mostly of determining project feasibility. Feasibility is where you determine if the project can make sense. Feasibility is the period when you conduct diligence. Diligence is the process of asking and answering all the questions that must be asked and answered to bring the project to a point where you decide it makes sense to move forward and build the project.

During feasibility there are many issues that must be addressed but there are six very important issues. These six issues are typically either fundamental to the project, very time consuming or very expensive.

The Pre-Development Phase, "Big Six" are:

1. Securing the land site.
2. Zoning, platting and other site and use issues.
3. Attracting tenants and users
4. Attracting financing partners; construction lender and equity investors.
5. Commissioning and completing architectural plans and specifications.
6. Permitting the project to build with the local municipality.

KEY PROFESSIONALS-
THE COMMERCIAL
REAL ESTATE BROKER.

It is no coincidence that we introduce the commercial real estate broker early in the process. Most real estate professionals will be able to answer all of the key questions outlined in this Guide especially questions related to the "Rule of Comps" and the "Big Six". The reason for this is simple; they are in the commercial market place every day doing real estate transactions helping to bring buyers and sellers together.

WehrVentures

STEP 9: The Development Phase and Identifying Comparable Land Sites

The Rule of Comps can be applied to almost every aspect of the CRE development process. Most developers early in the project will identify land comps. The land comps can help with negotiating a purchase price and other key terms. Other key terms like the time period needed to conduct diligence. To the developer, "time" may be more important than price. In Step 9, through internet research or working with a broker identify up to three comparable existing land sites that have sold or are for sale in the area of the project site. Determine the selling price or the asking price for each land parcel. The comparable land sites should be in close proximity to the targeted site or in similar sub-market with similar demographics, market characteristics, about the same size and preferably suitable for the same use.

STEP 10: The Development Phase and Zoning Process

Zoning is how a municipality controls the use of real property. In STEP 10 you must determine what the zoning designation is for the land site and if current zoning allows for the chosen product type and use. It is important to research both product type and use. For example the land site might be zoned for a restaurant (product type) but the zoning might not allow the use of serving alcohol (product use). If the zoning has to be changed research the process to change and how long it might take? Address the zoning and change process (if needed) in the development summary.

NOTE: Just about every municipality or jurisdiction has a land development web site where you can research zoning and other important information about the project and site. As part of Step 10 find the web site for the development agency where the site is located. If the land site is listed with a broker, the broker website should address many of the project specifics.

Step 11: The Development Phase and the Site Plat?

Platting is the process where the municipality determines how the new development will be part of and participate in the "subdivision" of surrounding area services. The plating process will identify how the new development must match up with the existing or planned utilities, roadways, drainage and other important items. The parcel size, lot & block, legal description and even the physical address are often defined in the platting process.

For Step 11 determine if the chosen land site is platted. If the parcel has to be platted research the platting process and determine how long it might take and how much it might cost? A new plat can take many months. Both zoning and platting are valid reasons to ask the land seller for more time or even a contingency to close in the feasibility period (defined in the letter of intent). Address the platting status and process, if needed in the development summary. NOTE: The properties broker can help you with zoning, platting and other land use issues. The development website of the local municipality can help with the research.

Step 12: The Development Phase and Other Land and Use Issues

Almost every municipality or jurisdiction has a land development web site where you can research zoning, platting and other important information about the project and site. Zoning and platting are just two of the very important land and use issues that must be explored. The goal for Step 12 is to make the developer aware of the numerous other land and use issues. This awareness is created by asking and answering key questions during the diligence. Key questions like how to deal with; large trees, easement's, environmental hazards, soils compatibility, historical preservation, wet lands, and numerous other land and use issues. See the next slide for a short, non-comprehensive list of other issues you should and will attempt to explore at some point during the development process. For Step 12 see how many of the following listed items you can address as they relate to your development project.

SEE THE WHAT SECTION OF THE PRINCIPLE BOOK AND CHAPTER 4 FOR SHORT DISCUSSION ON THE NUMEROUS "SURVEYS" AND "STUDIES" NEEDED.

STEP 12: (Cont'd.)

Some of the land and use issues typically explored during feasibility:

- Title Insurance Policy / commitment
- Legal site survey or "ALTA" survey
- Zoning Letter
- Easements to be Vacated
- Easements Required
- Ingress and Egress, Access and Curb Cut Approval
- Utility "Will Serve" Letters and surveys
    - Sanitary Sewer
    - Water, Domestic / Fire
    - Storm Drainage
    - Natural Gas
    - Electrical Service
    - Telephone
- Phase 1 Environmental Site Assessment Report
- Geologic Assessment
- Geotechnical Report
- Seismic Assessment Report
- Tree Preservation Plan/ Tree Protection and Replacement Plan
- Storm water Pollution Prevention Plan (SWPPP) or equivalent Erosion Control Plan
- Building Permit
- Property Owner's Association Approval
- Vested Rights

The list of issues that must be explored goes on and on don't forget the municipalities development web site where the project site is located to help with many of these issues.

SEE THE WHAT SECTION OF THE PRINCIPLES BOOK.

STEP 13: The Development Phase and the Land Purchase Price

For Step 13 you must determine a "presumed" purchase price or cost for the land site. If you have not negotiated with the seller of the land site for purposes of this Guide you can use the "average" asking price for the comps identified in Step 9. If no comps are identified you can always assume 100 percent of the sellers asking price. However, remember everything in commercial real estate is negotiable.

No matter what method you use to determine land sales price, remember for budgeting purposes to convert the purchase price to a "per square foot" dollar amount. In real estate almost every aspect of the development will be broken down to a, "cost, per square foot" basis. In most jurisdictions the land seller pays the relative brokerage commission for both the buyer and seller representative, typically, 4-6 percent of the selling price.

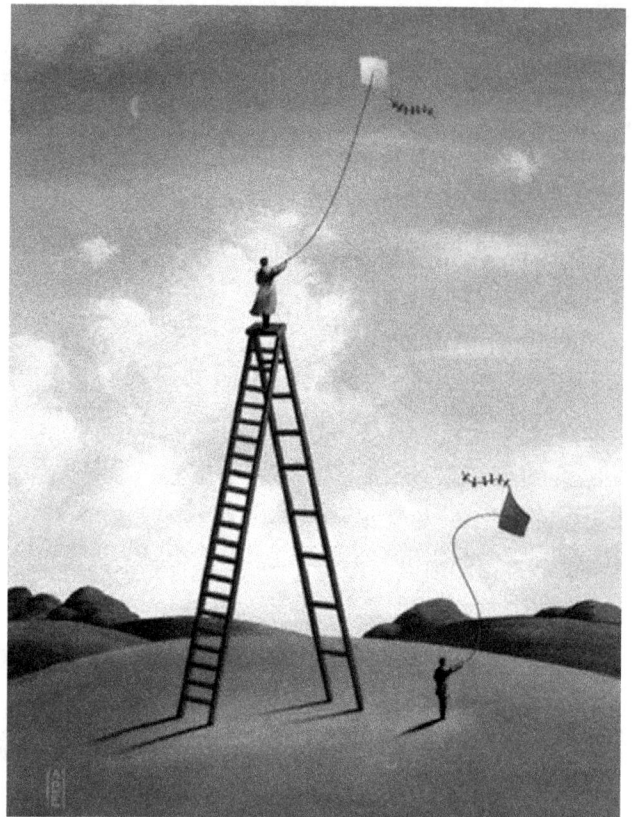

STEP 14: The Development Phase and Securing the Land for Purchase

At some point in the process you must secure the site for purchase. This is typically done in two stages. First entering into a Letter of Intent ("LOI") to purchase the land and second entering into an Earnest Money Contract ("EMC") or Purchase and Sale Agreement ("PSA"). In most jurisdictions the EMC or PSA is then deposited with a title company and the feasibility period begins. Once the PSA is deposited with the title company you have secured the right to purchase the land but not the obligation. You now have the entire feasibility period to conduct diligence. If you decide not to purchase the property during feasibility you will get your earnest money back. If you are participating in the development project a part of this Guide and interested in learning more you can go to the company's web site and download a simple LOI to purchase the land. Fill in the blanks with the material terms you believe our reasonable based on your market research. A commercial real estate broker can advise and draft the market terms outlined in a typical "LOI" to purchase land.

STEP 15: The Development Phase and Identifying Potential "Pre Leasing" Tenants

By studying the surrounding market, comparable buildings and competition, as well as researching the internet, talking with brokers, bankers and other developers you should be identifying what tenants to target for the project. If you are participating in the development exercise for Step 15 you will need to "arbitrarily" identify enough tenants that fit the vision for the project until you have 70 percent of the leasable space for the project leased. This Guide refers to these tenants as "financing" or "pre-leasing" tenants. They are referred to as financing tenants because the project financing partners typically require the project be pre-leased. This Guide uses 70 percent because this percentage of pre-leasing is well within the range of what most construction lender and equity investors will require to close the loan or invest.

SEE ATTACHMENT D FOR SAMPLES OF SIMPLE TENANT PRE-LEASING PLANS.

STEP 16: The Development Phase and Determining Lease Rate and Terms

The Rule of Comps can be utilized to determine a reasonable approach to almost every aspect of commercial real estate development. For Step 16 use the Rule of Comps to help outline various aspects of the tenant lease specifics including but not limited to the following: average lease rate, TI allowance, typical length of lease (in years) with tenants and even how long it took the comp project to fill up with tenants. For Step 16 you must determine the lease rate, lease term and TI allowance for the project. See the project assumptions page at the end of this Guide for more specific information.

For example: if the average advertised or existing lease rate for tenants leasing space in the comps is $20 PSF, you should model a lease rate between $16 (80 percent) and $24 (120 percent) depending on marketing research, strategy, product type and quality of your project. If the average TI of the comps was $25 PSF you can use $25 PSF as the TI allowance for the project pro forma and budget. If the average length of lease term of the comps is five years you can use five year for the project pro forma. As a general rule you can use the comp information to model project budget specifics.

STEP 17: The Development Phase: Terms with Pre-Leasing Tenants

The project construction lender and equity investors expect that you have negotiated and signed an LOI and even a lease agreement with many of the "financing" tenants before they will lend or invest. As pointed out in the previous steps this Guide assumes 70 percent of the tenants for leasable space3 have signed LOI's or leases before closing the construction loan and equity investment. The first step in putting together a lease agreement with tenants is often to enter into a Letter of Intent or "LOI". The LOI then acts as a guide for putting together the material terms of the lease agreement.

If your are interested in learning more please go to the Company's web site and download a simple tenant lease LOI. Fill out the LOI with the terms you discovered from the comp research. First, create an LOI for the most important financing tenant-the key tenant or anchor (if there is one). Keep in mind that anchors normally get better deals than the "shadow" or smaller surrounding tenants. You can source this information by researching the internet and talking to the project broker. Finally, if you participating in the development project complete an LOI for each of the 70 percent financing tenant's identified in Step 15.

STEP 18: The Development Phase: Identify the "Speculative" Tenants

In Step 15 you hypothetically identified tenants for 70 percent of the planned leasable space in your development project. That means there is another 30 percent of the building to lease. For the 70 percent "financing" tenants you plan to have a signed LOI and or lease agreement before closing on the project financing. If all goes as planned, these tenants move in and start paying rent when the building opens or as soon as the tenant finish out is completed. However, the remaining 30 percent only move in once tenants are identified, an LOI or the lease agreement is negotiated and signed and tenant build out is completed. This is why the unleased space in a development project is often referred to as "spec space" and tenants referred to "spec tenants". They are speculative, since the developer doesn't actually know when these tenants will be identified, sign leases and move-in and start paying rent.

In order to forecast how your development project might perform you must estimate when the spec tenants might be identified, move in and start paying rent. Remember you are early in the process of developing this commercial real estate project. You are attempting to model what you want to build and how it will be a success. A real estate broker familiar with the market can help you estimate how long it will take to fill up the "spec" space. If you know how long it took the comps to lease their spec space you can use this information. For Step 18 you must project what the leasing terms and specifics might be for the spec tenants. In addition you will need to outline over a period of time when the spec tenants might move-in and start paying rent. Do this until the building is completely leased. A fully leased building (90% or more) is often referred to as "stabilized".

STEP 19: The Development Phase: Identify Sale Comps

Sale comps for your development projects refer to projects that similar to what you want to build that have already been built, filled with tenants and sold. Sale comps and applicable cap rates are a valid measurement tool for what you might sell your project for once it is built and full of rent paying tenants. In Step 19 identify up to three comparable development projects, like the one you desire to build that have sold in the last twelve months. If available the projects should be within close proximity or in similar sub markets to your project location. Sale comps for similar projects can be identified through internet research, talking to brokers, building owners, bankers and other developers. Once project sale comps are identified determine the sales price and the "cap rate" that each sold for. NOTE: Don't forget project comps that are for sale in the general area of your project but have not yet sold. The offering price and cap rate is valuable comp information. Add a summary of the most important sales comps and the key information for each to your development summary.

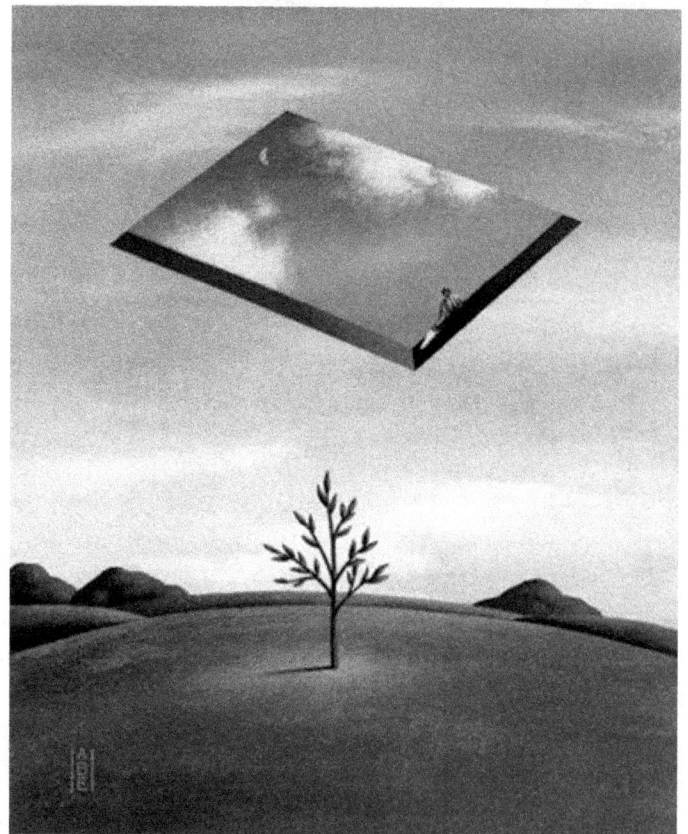

Definitions: Cap Rates

Cap rates for "comparable" properties are a convenient way to estimate the sale value for a real estate development project. Cap rates are the commercial real estate market's way of expressing the *long-term value* of the project's first full year's or "stabilized" cash flow over the life of the lease term. The important thing to remember is that dividing the first full year estimated NOI for the project by the historical market driven cap rate for similar projects (NOI/Cap Rate=Projected Sale Value) will help you determine what a buyer might pay for the project once built, full of tenants and ready for sale. Here are the important formulas:

- **Property Value= Net Operating Income/Cap Rate**
- Cap Rate= Net Operating Income (NOI)/Property Value
- Net Operating Income=Property Value x Cap Rate

NOTE: Remember you are using current information to determine value in a project not yet built and probably won't be for many years. This means you must spend some time researching where cap rates and overall values may be many years in the future. If developing real estate were easy everyone would be a commercial real estate developer!

SEE CHAPTER NINE OF THE PRINCIPLES BOOK.

STEP 20: The Development Phase: The Development Entity

The Internet is now the single most powerful tool to communicate to the world who you are and what you do. However, traditional communication and marketing tools are still very important and hard copy brochures, letterhead, and other fundamental business basics remain very important in presenting the developer and project plan. Fundamental business basics are now incorporated into traditional hard copy media but also into the digital technology, Web domain, and other Web media options. With this in mind you must begin thinking about the branding of the development company and project. For Step 20 you must select a name for your development company as well as initial legal structure for the development enterprise (see summary next slide). Finally, select a name for your development project and attempt to identify a website domain address for both the development entity and the project.

For Example the following is an initial press release copy demonstrating some of the above; *WehrOffice Ventures, L.L.C.* **(development company name and enterprise type)** *announced today it was building, "The Legacy",* **(development project name)** *a 34,500 SF, two story. office building on a 3.5 acre site at the corner of …….. More information can be found at www.legacyoffice.com* **(project website)** *or on our company website at www.wehrofficeventures.com ……*

It is important to understand that the business name, dot-com name, and the company trademark name are three separate and distinct names and assets.

SEE THE WHO SECTION OF THE PRINCIPLES BOOK FOR MORE INFORMATION ON NAMING RIGHTS AND LEGAL ENTITIES.

Definitions: Typical Legal Structures for Commercial Real Estate Developers

Limited Liability Company-A limited liability company or "LLC" is a unique mixture of the benefits of a corporation, including the corporate legal protection, and the ease and simplicity of a sole proprietorship. The LLC allows you to form a corporation but be treated for certain purposes as a sole proprietorship. *The LLC is a common form of ownership for developer entity and even the development project entity.*

Limited Partnership-Investors like the "LP" or "Ltd." enterprise structure when they decide to make an investment in a CRE project. The reason for this is found in the name—limited partnership. The basic distinction of a limited partnership or LP is to encourage investment by investors but to limit their personal exposure to any liability to their investment amount. *The LP and the LLC are both a common form of enterprise between the project developer and equity investor.*

"C" Corporation- A traditional corporate structure; Inc., Corp or Corporation is treated as if the entity is a person in and of itself, separate and distinct from the developer as an individual.

Sole Proprietorship- A sole proprietorship is merely a business run and operated through the developer as an individual.

See your States, Secretary of State office website, www.sos.state._____.us. for more information.

SEE THE WHO SECTION OF THE PRINCIPLES BOOK.

KEY PROFESSIONALS: THE COMPANY ATTORNEY OR LEGAL COUNSEL

Very early in the development process you will want to form a relationship with a real estate attorney. Almost every aspect of the four phases of commercial real estate development will involve important legal review, advise and drafting. You can rely on counsel for insight and negotiation through all four phases of the development process and negotiations with all the key players.

Here are just a few of the important areas legal counsel can be helpful: LOI and PSA for the project land, review of the title policy and ALTA survey and other key land and use issues, LOI and negotiation of the lease agreement with all tenants, AIA agreement with architect and general contractor, LOI and lending agreement with the construction lender, initial development company corporate structure, LOI and investment documents with the equity investors. The list goes on and on. Form a relationship early in the development company cycle with a competent real estate lawyer.

STEP 21: The Development Phase: Create a Project Summary

For Step 21 assemble a project summary. The project summary is just a brief synapsis of the information you have assembled related to the project. The project summary is a very helpful tool to help explain the project to others, like future potential tenants and financing partners. Keep adding to the summary as you gather, receive and solidify additional information during the diligence and feasibility period.

SEE ATTACHMENT E FOR A SAMPLE OF AN INITIAL PROJECT SUMMARY.

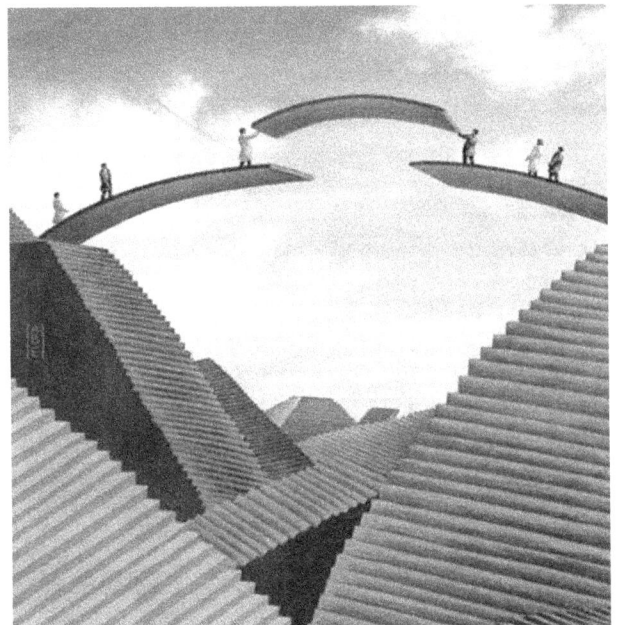

TIP #5: The Project Financials and the, "Three Legged Stool"

There comes a time during the project feasibility period that you must determine if the project makes sense. The why principle. Why does this project make sense and why should banks and investors give you their money. Putting together a financial picture is a very important step in demonstrating the potential success of the project and getting lenders to lend and investors to invest. This author likes to think that modeling the financials for a commercial real estate project is analogous to a "three legged stool". The seat or platform is the project plan and summary. The three legs of the stool are the support structure. The three legs of the stool represent three key financial areas you must address in the project pro forma:

1. Project Operations
2. Project Cost
3. Project Profit

WehrVentures

PART 3: PROJECT OPERATIONS

Why Should the Lender, Lend and
the Equity Investor, Invest?

TIP #6: Look at The Project Like a Business

A real estate development project can be thought of as two very distinct businesses. The first business is the business of converting a vision into an actual commercial real estate project that gets built and tenants moved in and paying rent.

The second business is the business of operating and managing the completed project. The important thing to remember is you must analyze both aspects of the business to determine if the project you envision can be a success. From the developer's perspective there are three key areas related to operating the business that the developer must forecast and make a part of the financial pro forma:

1. Gross Revenue
2. Net Operating Income
3. Value of project upon sale or refinance

FOR ADDITIONAL INFORMATION SEE THE AUTHORS ARTICLE, "TEN SIMPLE STEPS TO ESTIMATE PROJECT SUCCESS" AVAILABLE ON THE COMPANY WEB SITE.

STEP 22: Project Operations: Rent Roll and Lease-up Pro Forma

Early in the development process you must begin to convert the vision to "numbers". The numbers are a snapshot of how you think the project will perform. Can the project make money? Using a financial spread sheet (visit the company web site for a spread sheet that can be downloaded) create an estimated rent roll and lease-up schedule.

The rent roll and lease up is basically your projection over a period of time (probably a couple of years) that outlines when you believe the tenants move-in and start paying rent. The rent roll and lease-up schedules are the developer's best estimate of what the financial terms with each of the tenants will be and when the tenants will move into the project. This information can be obtained by studying the comps. If the estimated lease rate, lease term and lease-up time information is not available from the comps a broker can give you an estimate.

NOTE: If you don't have this information for purposes of the development project ASSUME the building will be leased up or "stabilized" two years from when you think the building will first open. See the assumptions page at the end of this Guide for more specific information.

SEE ATTACHMENT F FOR EXAMPLE OF A PROJECT OPERATIONAL FINANCIAL SUMMARY INCLUDING RENT ROLL AND LEASE-UP PRO FORMA. SEE ALSO CHAPTER EIGHT OF THE PRINCIPLES BOOK.

WehrVentures

STEP 23: Project Operations: Estimate Gross Revenue

To estimate gross revenue for the project multiply the average estimated rent rate by the project total "leasable" space.

For example: Let's ASSUME the "average" market lease rate for project in the area is @$20 per sq. ft., "triple net". You believe this is a reasonable average lease rate for the 30,000 rentable square footage project you want to build. A $20 "triple net" lease rate times 30,000 sq. ft., appears capable of generating $600,000 ($20 X 30,000) in annual gross revenue once stabilized (full of rent paying tenants).

For Step 23 and the project financial pro forma you will need to estimate gross revenue for each individual lease agreement with tenants to rent space in the project. Enter this information into the project financial summary.

SEE ATTACHMENT F FOR PROJECT EXAMPLE ESTIMATING GROSS REVENUE.

WehrVentures

Definitions: Vacancy Factor

Most developers, construction lenders and equity investors will discount or offset the estimated gross rental income for one or all of the following three things: tenant credit risk, project capital expenditures and vacancy factor. *Credit Risk* is just an assessment of the creditworthiness of the tenant—will they pay the rent as due or default and break the lease. *Capital expenses* are expenses not typically reimbursed or covered in triple net costs paid by the tenant. Costs like; responsibility for the roof, support walls and foundation. Finally, most construction lenders and equity investors will input a vacancy factor. The *vacancy factor* is a way to account for delay, turnover and actual vacancy in the project. The vacancy factor is typically determined as a small percent of total rentable square footage typically, 5-10 percent.

SEE CHAPTER EIGHT OF THE PRINCIPLES BOOK.

STEP 24: Project Operations: Estimate Net Operating Income ("NOI")

This Guide ASSUMES all leases with tenants are "triple net" (NNN). Triple net leases pass through to the tenant their pro rata share of the operating expenses (typically based on square footage leased to total square footage in building). The tenant pays these pro rata expenses as additional rent to the developer each month. This additional rent is typically adjusted each year based on actual prior year expenses for the building. Thus the effect when the building has stabilized or "leased-up" and all leases are "NNN" is that all the operating expenses are effectively paid by the tenants.

Since this Guide ASSUMES all leases are "NNN" gross base rent revenue will pass through to become the net income. However, we must still account for the three factors discussed in the vacancy factor slide. If you are participating in the development exercise multiply net income by 90 percent ($600,000 X .90 = $540,000). This represents a 10 percent vacancy/credit risk/capital discount factor. Enter the discounted amount into pro forma as the project net operating income. If you are developing a product type that traditionally does not utilize the "NNN" lease approach (like apartments) you will need to study the comps for operating expense information and add this operating cost to the pro forma.

SEE ATTACHMENT F AND CHAPTER EIGHT IN THE PRINCIPLES BOOK.

Definitions: List of Typical Lease Types Entered into with Tenants

- **GROSS LEASE:** A gross lease or "pass-through" lease means the landlord will pay for certain expenses like maintenance, taxes, and insurance and the tenant only pays a base rent to the Landlord.

- **TRIPLE NET LEASE:** The most common type of net lease is the *triple net lease* ("NNN"). With a triple net lease, the tenant pays as additional rent (on top of the base rent) their pro rata share of building taxes, insurance, management and maintenance cost. The pro rate share of expenses is typically determined as a percent of the total rentable square footage the tenant has leased to the total rentable square footage in the building. There can also be add-on factors (additional rent) for project common areas.

- **MODIFIED GROSS LEASE:** a modified gross lease falls somewhere in between a NNN lease and a gross lease. In the modified gross lease the landlord may agree to pay for certain expenses like real property taxes and major repairs (roof, foundation), but the tenant might be responsible for others such as insurance and minor repairs.

- **BASE YEAR LEASE:** Another approach to dealing with expenses is for the tenant to pay for all increases of certain expenses over the base year. For example if the property tax increases after the first year the landlord would pass this increase to the tenant.

Lease types should not be confused with a building "add-on or "load factor". A building add-on or load factor is the way the developer charges tenants for the use and enjoyment of the building common areas.

SEE CHAPTER EIGHT OF THE PRINCIPLES BOOK FOR MORE INFORMATION ON ADD-ON OR LOAD FACTOR CALCULATIONS.

STEP 25: Project Operations: Estimate Gross Value of Project Upon Sale

Once you have determined the estimated net operating income or NOI for the project you can estimate what a buyer might pay for the project. To estimate the project sale value divide the first full year NOI by the average cap rate of the comps. The first year NOI is the first full twelve months your pro forma projects the project will be leased-up. You want to use the first twelve month period the project is stabilized because this helps you maximize the NOI. A maximized NOI will drive a greater sale value. The NOI divided by the applicable cap rate (stated as a percent) will result in a projected sale value (NOI/average cap rate of comps equals' estimated gross valve upon sale). Don't forget these financials are projections. It is important to research the internet to find out where cap rates might be a few years from now when the project is full of tenants and ready to sell.

If the project is a 30,000 rentable square foot office building with estimated first full year (stabilized) NOI of $540,000 and the average cap rate for comparable buildings that sold in the last twelve months was 8 percent, the projected sale value for the project at an "8 cap" would be $6,750,000 ($540,000/.08).

SEE ATTACHMENT F AND SEE CHAPTER EIGHT AND NINE IN THE PRINCIPLES BOOK.

STEP 26: Project Operations: Estimate NET Value of Project Upon Sale

All commercial real estate transactions incur cost and expenses. Expenses like; legal fees, commissions and closing costs. For STEP 26 you must estimate these costs and expenses and net them from the gross sale proceeds. For purposes of this Guide and your development summary (unless you have more accurate information) ASSUME 5-10% of the estimated project sales value for commissions, fees and closing cost, including legal.

For example if the project estimated sale value is $6,750,000 ($540,000/.08) subtract 7 percent or @$500,000 (rounded up slightly-remember we are estimating) for Brokerage commission, closing cost and expenses. The net Value of project upon sale for this example is @$6,250,000.

NOTE: The 5-10% is obviously an estimate and not a hard rule. Talk to local brokers and research the internet or rely on the comp information to estimate the cost of closing for the type of project you are planning to build and sell.

SEE ATTACHMENT F AND CHAPTER EIGHT OF THE PRINCIPLES BOOK.

Part 4: PROJECT COST

Why Should the Construction Lender, Lend and the Equity Investor, invest?

TIP #7: Estimating Total Project Cost

There are five basic costs to estimate in almost every commercial real estate project. Remember you are early in the development process and trying to determine if the project might be feasible. Therefore estimating certain costs is a lot less expensive than actually engaging the professionals and incurring these costs. Keep in mind the application of the Rule of Comps when estimating each of the basic costs. The five basic costs are:

1. Land cost
2. Construction or "HARD" costs.
3. Design and other "SOFT" costs.
4. Tenant improvement/brokerage commission costs.
5. Financing or construction loan costs.

KEY PROFESSIONALS: THE GENERAL CONTRACTOR

The general contractor or "GC" or construction manager or "CM" is the entity that enters into a contract with the developer for the purpose of constructing the project. The general contractor is responsible for organization of the entire construction team, project schedule, safety, and all processes that lead to a completed building or project in compliance with the architectural plans and specs.

The GC should establish a responsibility matrix, milestone schedule, site utilization plan, and construction documents, choose the subs, manage each discipline, and oversee the bid and coordination of purchasing, delivery, and installation of equipment and supplies. The GC will also help coordinate and prepare draw request to the budget or what is known as the schedule of values. Finally the GC will help create process for change order review and approval and incorporate all of these and other issues and functions into the overall construction scheme, budget, and construction schedule. The schedule is important in helping you know when the tenants can be moved in and start paying rent.

Go to AIA.org and review or download a standard "GMAX" contract between the owner and a GC. Most bank lenders and equity investors will expect a GMAX contract between the you and your contractor.

STEP 27: Project Cost: Estimate Construction or "Hard" Cost

In STEP 27 you must estimate the construction or hard costs for the project. Hard cost construction estimates should include; off-site and on-site costs and all core and shell construction costs. (See Chapter 7 in the Principles Book for understanding of on-site, offsite and core and shell costs).

There are sources on the internet that publish annual cost per square foot estimates for different commercial real estate product types. You can also talk to the project broker or meet with a general contractor familiar with the project type to get the hard cost estimates for the project. The contractors who built the comps identified in previous steps should be able to give you construction cost estimates for your project. The GC will give you cost estimates for gross square footage. (exterior wall to exterior wall) The estimate from the GC will likely be to deliver a, "cold shell" or "cold white box". The tenant TI allowance is the landlord or developer source of funds to take the space from cold shell or cold white box to usable space.

SEE ATTACHMENT F FOR EXAMPLE OF COST OR BUDGET INCLUDING HARD COST OR CONSTRUCTION BUDGET. SEE ALSO CHAPTER 7 OF THE PRINCIPLES BOOK.

Cold shell - a building with minimal interior finish out.

Cold white box - a building which may include some or all of the following; ceilings, lighting, plumbing, interior walls, elevator, rest rooms, concrete floor.

Warm shell or vanilla shell - should include everything listed above for the cold white box but also include HVAC (heating, ventilation and air conditioning system).

The developer will typically leave each floor in "shell" condition to be built out as tenants are identified. Once tenants are actually identified and the building is constructed the space can be built-out to fit the tenant requirement.

STEP 28: Project Cost: Estimate Design Costs

Architectural design services can be very expensive. You want to make an initial determination that the project is feasible before incurring these soft costs. Early in the development process you can estimate design cost by assuming these costs will be a percentage of the construction cost. If you are participating in the development exercise you can assume between 5-10 percent of total hard costs for architectural and design related soft costs. For the final cost analysis you will need to engage an architect. The architect, once engaged, will develop the project design embodied in the plans and specs or drawings. In many instances the architects plans and specs will also include certain civil engineering cost. You then use these drawings to bid out and choose a GC. The GC will then use the plans and specs to bid out and cost the project.

For example if the GC quotes you $125 a foot for 34,500 GSF the estimated construction cost is $4,310,000. If you take 7% of this cost the estimated architectural and design cost would be @$300,000. For purposes of this Guide and for Step 28 ASSUME a range of 5-10 percent of total hard cost to estimate design related soft costs for your project.

SEE ATTACHMENT F FOR EXAMPLE OF ITEMIZED SOFT COSTS AND PRO FORMA FOR BUDGETING SOFT COST AND CHAPTER SEVEN OF THE PRINCIPLES BOOK.

STEP 29: Project Cost: Estimating Remaining "Soft" Costs

There are other soft costs that need to be estimated other than architectural design costs. The developer's fee for example is considered a soft cost. The development fee is typically 3-6% of total project cost; including hard cost, architectural and engineering, other soft costs (sometimes land). There are also numerous others soft cost beyond the developer fee. Cost such as; insurance, title cost, marketing, utility fees, legal fees etc. and sometimes a contingency (for unplanned or unanticipated expenses). It is difficult to say what the percentage might be because it can vary widely by jurisdiction but for this Guide ASSUME an additional 5- 10 percent of hard costs for the remaining additional soft costs.

For Step 29 if you ASSUME an additional 7 percent or $300,000 for all remaining soft costs. This would give you a total of $600,000 in soft costs. If you are participating in the development process for Step 29 calculate this amount for your project and include in the estimated project budget under "other" soft costs.

SEE ATTACHMENT F FOR EXAMPLE OF A SOFT COST BUDGET.

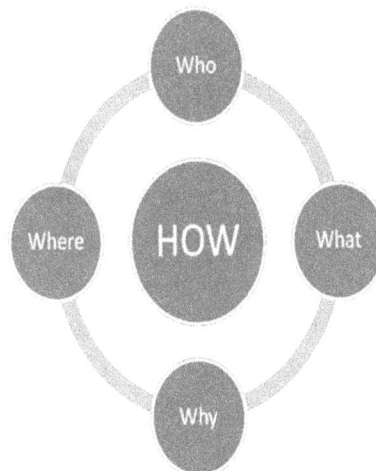

STEP 30: Project Cost: Estimate Developer TI Allowance Cost

You have now estimated three of the five basic costs; land cost, construction or hard costs and design and other soft costs. In STEP 30 you need to budget for landlord or developer funded tenant improvement cost. When researching the comps you collected, amongst other things information related to landlord or developer funded project tenant improvement or TI allowance. Utilizing this information for Step 30 calculate the estimated total TI dollars that you will need to budget.

Lets assume a majority of developer/landlords in the surrounding market for the project comps are giving $20 per rentable square foot TI allowance. If your project has 30,000 RSF and you assume $20 TI allowance then the total TI dollars is $600,000.($20 X 30,000 RSF). The $600,000 becomes the amount you put in the pro forma or budget for TI allowance. The tenant is typically responsible to fund any additional monies needed to finish out the space.

Apartments, hotels and other, "build it and the tenants will come" development product types typically build the "TI" costs into the hard cost construction budget.

SEE ATTACHMENT F FOR EXAMPLE.

STEP 31: Project Cost: Estimate Brokerage Commission Cost

Another significant expense that must be budgeted is the potential leasing commissions. The approach to calculating brokerage leasing commissions can vary by jurisdiction. For budgeting purposes you should estimate commission for all leasable space in your project. For STEP 31, and for purposes of this Guide if you don't know the typical market commission in your area ASSUME 6% brokerage lease commissions on all leasable space. The brokerage commission for a signed lease agreement is typically calculated on the total revenue that will be generated during the base or initial term of a lease times the appropriate commission percentage.

For example, if the tenant has entered into a five year lease for 10,000 square feet at $20 PSF rent the estimated commission would be; 10,000 ($20) =$200,000; $200,000 (5yrs) =$1,000,000 (6 percent) =$60,000. The total payable commission in this example is $60,000.

The commission percentage in many markets is a total of 6 percent and typically allocated; 4 percent to tenant broker and 2 percent to the developer/landlord, broker. Commissions are often payable as follows: one half at lease signing and one half when the tenant moves in and starts paying rent. In many jurisdictions there are commissions payable on additional rent amounts. Additional commissions may be payable on Items like triple net reimbursements, lease renewals and sometimes lease expansions. For Step 31 determine the projected commission for each lease in your project, total these amounts and add to the project budget.

SEE ATTACHMENT F FOR EXAMPLE.

TIP #8: The "Fixer Upper"; Rehabbing an Existing Project

Attracting rent-paying tenants remains the most important aspect of any commercial real estate development, whether you are building a new building or buying and rehabbing an existing building. Once the developer has tenants interested in leasing the building, finding the financing to purchase and rehab will be much easier. So how does a developer reasonably assess and analyze the true "all in" cost of purchasing and rehabbing an existing commercial building or project?

There are five major cost issues that you must address to assess the overall investment in purchasing and rehabbing an existing commercial building. These five costs are; 1) the purchase price of the building, 2) the cost of basic rehabilitation and repair, 3) the cost to make the space attractive or suitable for the intended or targeted tenants and users, 4) the tenant improvement cost or landlord tenant improvement allowance, and 5) the real estate brokerage commissions (and other costs, fees and expenses). Understanding these five costs will help you evaluate the real cost of acquiring the project and determine if the investment makes good economic sense.

Of course you are likely to borrow some of the money needed to purchase and rehab an existing building so don't forget the cost of financing!

Definitions: Loan Terms with Construction Lender

Early in the development process you must also estimate the cost of the construction loan. Construction loans are interest only during construction and for a short time thereafter. Therefore you must estimate the interest payments to the lender during the construction period and until the debt is paid off. Once you estimate loan interest cost these cost get added to the development budget. To estimate these costs you can research the internet, talk with a broker and or meet with commercial banks making real estate development construction loans.

For budgeting purposes and to estimate loan cost you will need to know the following basic loan terms.
1.) Construction loan interest rate and whether fixed or floating.
2.) Percentage of loan amount the lender will lend to total project cost.
3.) The time period when loan must be paid off.
4.) Fees and expenses for loan review and approval.
5.) PERSONAL GUARANTEE FROM THE DEVELOPER!

NOTE: Construction loans are typically short term. The term of the loan is just long enough to get the project built, tenants moved in and paying rent and a short time thereafter. Most construction lenders will make available a more permanent or "take out" loan when they agree to do a short term construction loan. The longer term loan is often referred to as a "mini-perm". This "mini perm" loan is used to replace the construction loan when the construction loan matures. The bank will also commission an appraisal be done on the proposed development project. The appraisal process will take a hard look at how your proposed project compares to the market comps and market driven terms. Another good reason to understand and follow the "Rule of Comps".

STEP 32: Project Cost: Construction Loan Interest Costs

Construction loans are interest only during construction and for short term thereafter. In addition construction loans are funded monthly, as you need the money to buy and build. Therefore the loans are not really fully funded until the end of construction. Because of this, the *average outstanding principal balance* at any point in time can be difficult to estimate without a financial calculator. The outstanding balance is needed for purposes of determining the total interest to be paid. For STEP 32 you need to estimate the total loan interests to be paid and other loan costs like fees and expenses. Use a financial calculator and calculate the estimated interest expense by applying the project specifics to the loan terms.

If you don't have a financial calculator or other tool here is a simple approach that can help you estimate interest expense for a construction loan:

1. Estimate total project cost and multiply it by the loan-to-cost limitation (ASSUME 70 percent). The product of these two items is the estimated construction loan amount.

2. Take the estimated construction loan amount times 50 percent. The product of this step is the assumed average outstanding balance amount estimate.

3. Take the assumed average outstanding balance estimate times the interest rate your market research or lender has indicated the bank will charge.

4. Take the product of this amount times the estimated time to construct, lease up and sell the finished product-in years (1.5 or 2.0 etc.). The estimated time can be derived by studying the comps. This amount is your estimated interest expense.

5. Finally add an additional 2.5-5% of the loan amount to estimate fees and expenses to close the construction loan.

   Add the interest expense and fees amount to the project budget.

SEE ATTACHMENT F FOR EXAMPLE AND SEE CHAPTER SEVEN OF THE PRINCIPLES BOOK.

STEP 33: Project Cost: Calculate Total Project Cost

You have now or estimated all five of the basic development costs for a commercial real estate project:

1. Land cost, see Step 13.

2. Construction or hard costs see Step 27.

3. Design and other soft costs, see Step 28 & 29.

4. Tenant improvement and lease commission costs, see Step 30 & 31.

5. Construction loan interest cost and fees, see Step 32.

The sum of all these five costs should give you a fair estimate of total project cost.

For STEP 33 add these costs together and determine estimated total project cost. Enter these amounts into the development project budget pro forma.

Part 5: PROJECT PROFIT

Why Should the Construction Lender, Lend and the Equity Investor, Invest?

TIP #9: Four Questions Equity Investors Want Answered

To calculate the potential project profit you must be able to answer four basic questions. The four basic questions that every equity investor in a commercial real estate development project wants answered are:

1. How much money do you want me to invest?

2. How long will the money be invested?

3. Will any money be distributed during the investment?

4. How much money can I reasonably expect to get upon sale or refinance of the project?

SEE THE HOW SECTION OF THE PRINCIPLES BOOK FOR DISCUSSION ON LEGAL STRUCTURE BETWEEN THE EQUITY INVESTOR AND DEVELOPER.

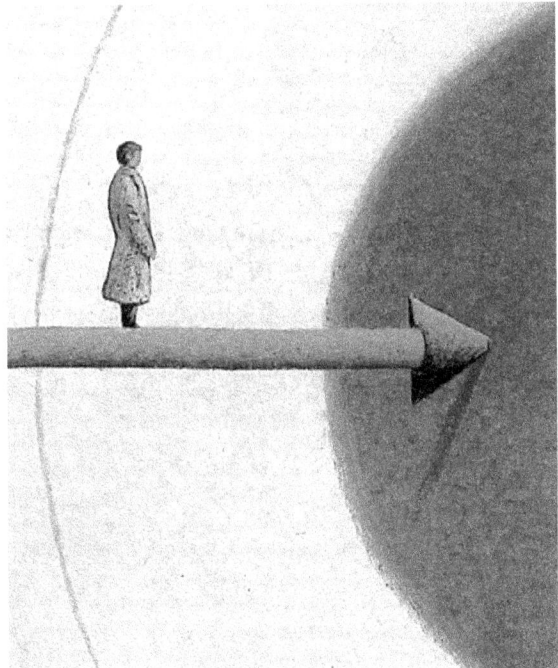

STEP 34: Project Profit: Equity Investment Amount

As part of this Guide you ASSUME that the construction lender will lend 70 percent of total project cost. If 70 percent of project cost is the construction loan then you must raise 30 percent of total project cost from equity (the remaining amount) to be able to fund your commercial real estate project.

For example if total project cost is estimated to be $5 million dollars then using the 70/30 formula set up by this Guide, the construction lender will lend you $3.5 million dollars. Therefore you must raise $1.5 million dollars from the equity investors.

For Step 34 you must estimate how much money you need the equity investor to invest. Keep in mind that the equity investor will likely require that you, the developer fund some of the equity required. It is not unusual in a commercial real estate development project for the equity investors to expect the developer to fund up to 10 percent of total equity needed. In our example 10 percent of $1,500,000 is $150,000! In this example if the developer invests equity of $150,000 the primary equity will need to invest $1,350,000.

SEE CHAPTER NINE OF THE PRINCIPLES BOOK FOR DISCUSSION OF EQUITY AND THE DEVELOPER CO-INVESTMENT.

STEP 35: Project Profit: How long will Equity be Invested (and will any Cash be Distributed during Investment)?

The construction lender will require that the equity investment be "first in" or, first invested. With this in mind you can assume that the time the equity will be invested will be from the time you close the construction loan to the time the finished commercial real estate project is sold or refinanced. Your contractor or broker can help you estimate how long this might take. For modeling purposes ASSUME equity is invested in year "zero" or the first day the time period begins to run.

For example If you are building a 30,000 RSF two story, Class B, office building your contractor might advise you it should take about 9 months to complete construction and receive a Certificate of Occupancy or "C of O". Since you have completed your lease up schedule and rent roll you have an estimate of how long it should take you to fill up the building with rent paying tenants. For purposes of this Guide use either the projected build time and lease-up estimate or ASSUME 2 years from estimated date of C of O. With the time to construct and the time to fill the building with tenants you have determined most of the time needed. However you will probably need a few additional months to manage, operate and market the project for sale. If you don't have an estimated market driven time for purposes of this Guide ASSUME 3-6 months.

You now have estimated the investors' money will be invested for approximately 3 years before an event of sale might occur; 9 months to build 2 years or 24 months to fill the building with rent paying tenants and finally 3 months to arrange for sale or refinance. For STEP 35 estimate how long the equity investor's money will be invested in your project.

For purposes of this Guide you can ASSUME no cash is distributed during the equity investment period. For budgeting purposes ASSUME excess cash generated, if any is used to pay down the construction loan.

ATTACHMENT F FOR EXAMPLE OF CALCULATING PROJECT PROFIT AND CHAPTER NINE OF THE

PRINCIPLES BOOK.

STEP 36: Project Profit: Investor Expectation upon Sale?

Most equity investors that invest in new commercial real estate developments expect internal rate of return (IRR) in the 15-25% range. It is typical for equity investors in commercial real estate investments to achieve the IRR by being paid the following:

1. A cumulative preferred or "pref" (interest rate) is paid on the equity invested for the time invested until paid back. Research the internet and talk with other developers or local broker to determine the market pref being offered for the product type. Typically the pref is between 6-12 percent. For purposes of this Guide if you don't have a market driven pref use an 8 percent pref for equity invested.

2. Upon a sale or refinancing the "pref" is paid and then typically all invested equity is paid back to the investors (including you, the developer for your invested equity).

3. Once the pref is paid and all the invested equity retuned to the investors and developer the parties split the remaining profit or the "promote" as agreed to in the original partnership agreement. There is often a minimum threshold return to the primary investor before the developer participates at this level.

For Step 36 you must determine the potential IRR for the equity investor.

The combination of these three payments; pref, return of principle (time value of money) and profit or promote should result in a projected IRR to the equity investor in the 15-25% range. For purposes of this Guide you can

ASSUME the profit or promote is split 70/30, seventy percent (70) to the investor and 30 percent to you, the developer.

SEE CHAPTER NINE OF THE PRINCIPLES BOOK FOR EXAMPLE OF EQUITY DEAL RETURN.

STEP 37: Project Profit: The Project "Waterfall"

When a commercial real estate project is sold or refinanced the proceeds are typically distributed as follows:

1. Pay off the construction loan.

2. Pay the expenses of the sale or refinance transaction.

3. Distribute or pay the accrued "pref" to the investors.

4. Pay back invested equity to each investor.

5. Split the remaining profit or "promote" as outlined in the agreement between you and the investor. For purposes of this Guide you can ASSUME; 70/30 split between the investor and developer.

The distribution of cash upon a sale or refinance is often referred to as the "waterfall". For Step 37 create a "waterfall" for your project proceeds upon sale or refinance.

SEE EXAMPLE F FOR EXAMPLE OF WATERFALL AND CHAPTER NINE OF THE PRINCIPLES BOOK.

STEP 38: Project Profit: Equity Return on Investment

The entire development process is a series of negotiations. In light of this you will constantly need to change, modify or update the many key factors of the development project. You will do this for numerous reasons but one reason is to demonstrate if the project can perform within the expectation of the investors (15 - 25 percent IRR). Of course, the project must also meet your goals and objectives. Remember everything in commercial real estate development is negotiable and messaging or moving the many variables around to see if the deal makes sense is part of the process. For STEP 38 if your project is not demonstrating at least a 15 percent IRR or if the pro forma is demonstrating return over 25 percent IRR to the investors adjust and work with any or all of the parameters set forth in this Guide to see if the project can be made more typical for you as the developer and the various parties involved.

SEE ATTACHMENT F FOR EXAMPLE OF IRR

(DEAL RETURN) CALCULATION FOR EQUITY INVESTOR & DEVELOPER.

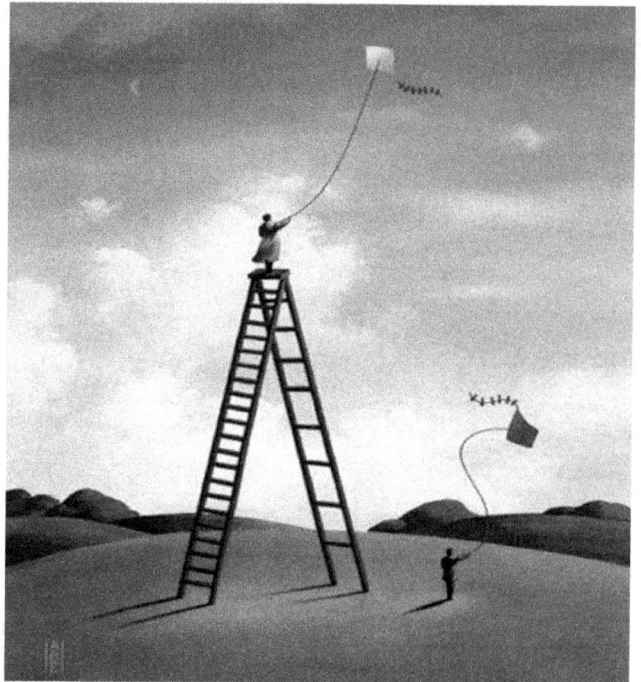

STEP 39: Complete an Initial Financial Plan

In addition to a final Project Summary you will want to complete an initial financial plan. At a minimum, the financial plan should address the three key areas as discussed in the previous slides:

1. Total Project Cost or budget (five key costs).
2. Operating pro forma; revenue, expenses, net operating income and sale value.
3. Profit or promote potential and distribution of proceeds or waterfall (deal return).

Most investors and construction lenders will want to see a Sources and Uses table as well as other key metrics.

For Step 39 create a Financial Plan for the Project.

SEE CHAPTER TEN OF THE PRINCIPLES BOOK AND PLEASE VISIT THE COMPANY WEB SITE FOR SAMPLES OF COMPLETED PROJECT FINANCIAL PLANS A PART OF THE PROJECT PLANS EXAMPLES.

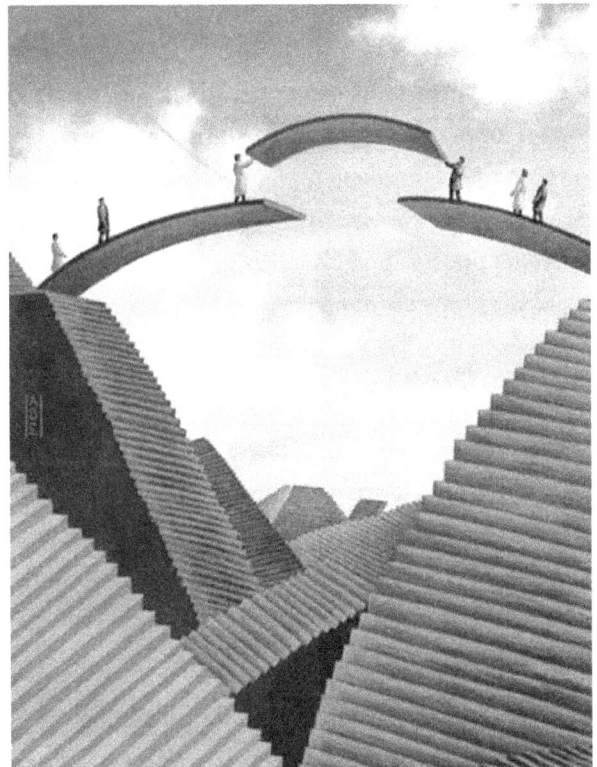

STEP 40: Complete an Initial Project Plan

The final Project Plan (and financial plan) must ask and answer all of the diligence questions and reasonably demonstrate the project is feasible and therefore worth your time, effort and money. For the final step you must put all the information together in a form others can understand and appreciate. Hopefully you have been adding to the project summary as you have addressed the many steps outlined in this Guide.

In Step 40 complete an initial Project Plan by adding the information compiled and any other pertinent information you may have. Keep in mind the Project Plan will almost certainly change as you learn more about each aspect of the project and the project moves closer and closer to closing the investment and loan, pulling the permits and construction of the project.

SEE THE HOW SECTION OF THE PRINCIPLES BOOK AND PLEASE VISIT OUR COMPANY WEB SITE FOR ACCESS TO SAMPLES OF COMPLETED PROJECT PLANS.

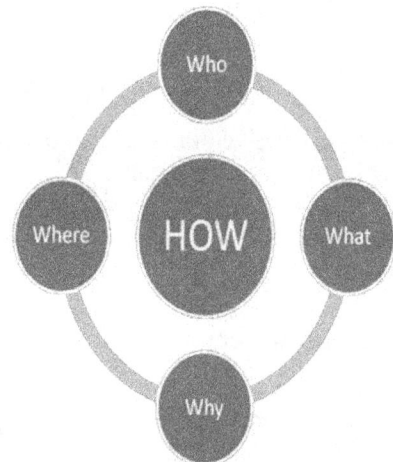

TIP #10: Three Keys to Developing Commercial Real Estate

This Guide and the Principles Book are based on the simple premise that there are three keys to developing commercial real estate.

The three keys are:

1. Location attracts tenants

2. Tenants sign leases and pay rent

3. Rent attracts financing (both equity investors and construction lenders).

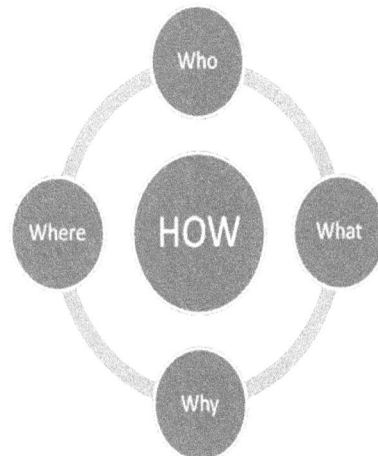

ATTACHMENTS

Attachment A: Location Map Samples

Attachment B: Simple Site Plans

Attachment C: Picture, Drawing or Rendering

Attachment D: Simple Tenant Pre-Leasing Plans

Attachment E: Initial Project Summary Sample

Attachment F: Project; Cost, Operations and Profit

To view additional samples of the Attachments visit our web sites: www.developingcre.com or www.wehrventures.com

WehrVentures

Attachment A: Location Map Samples

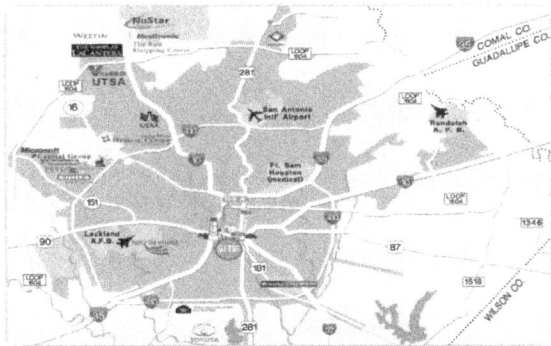

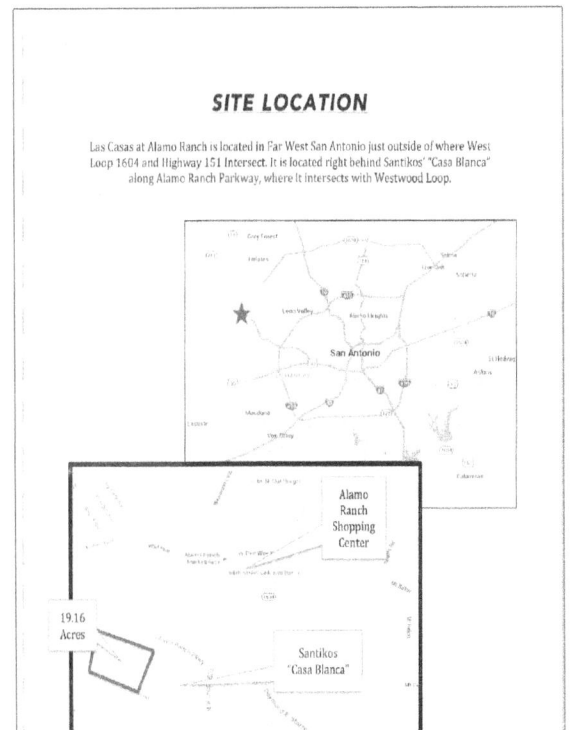

SITE LOCATION

Las Casas at Alamo Ranch is located in Far West San Antonio just outside of where West Loop 1604 and Highway 151 intersect. It is located right behind Santikos' "Casa Blanca" along Alamo Ranch Parkway, where it intersects with Westwood Loop.

Attachment B: Simple Site Plans

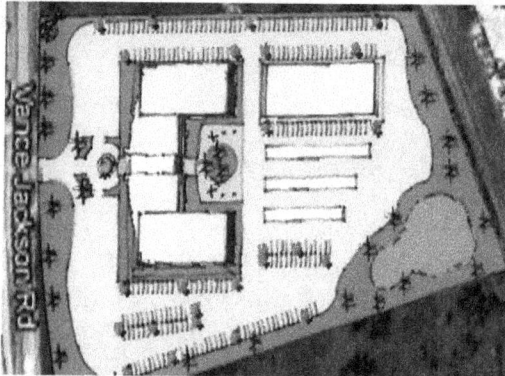

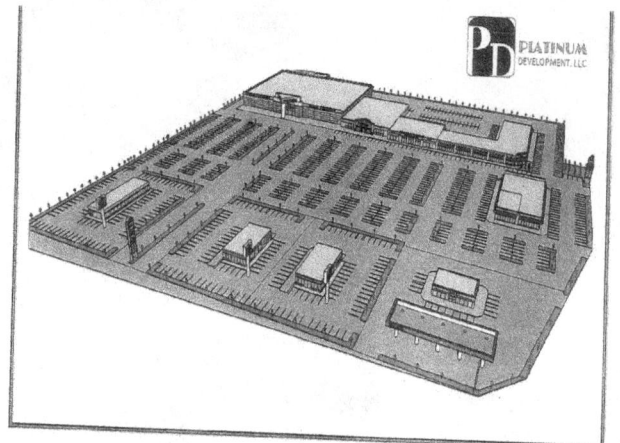

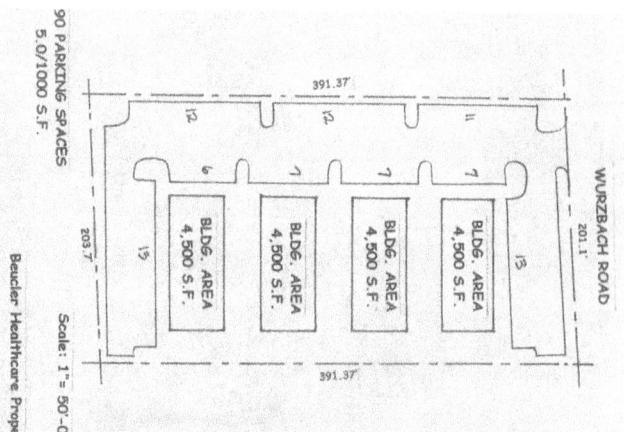

Attachment C: Picture, Drawing or Rendering

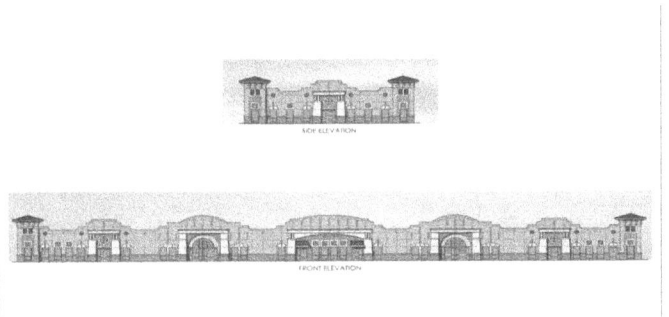

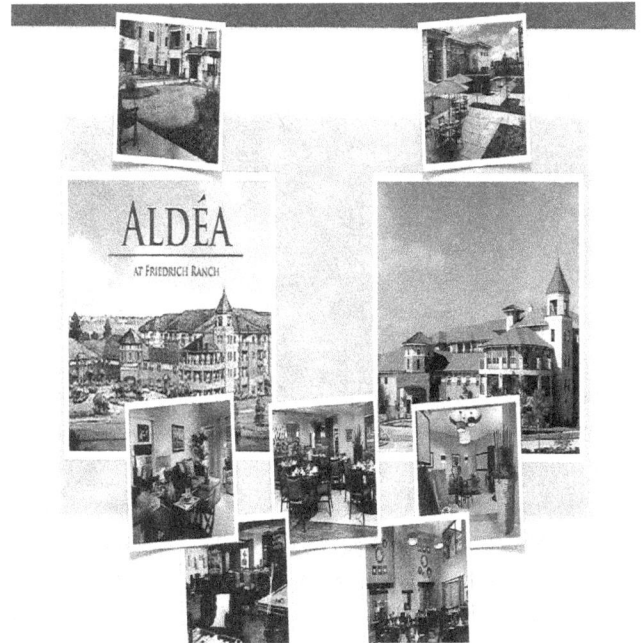

Attachment D: Tenant Pre-Leasing Plans

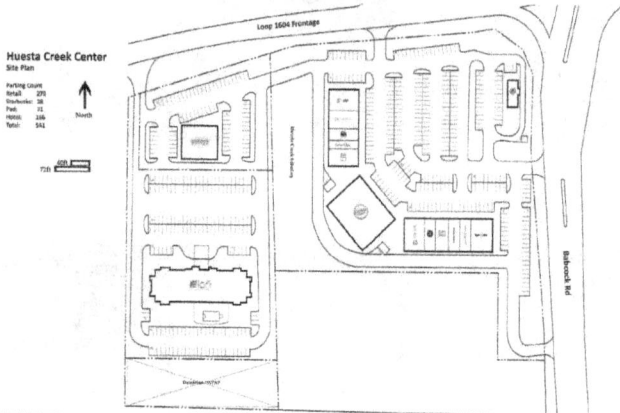

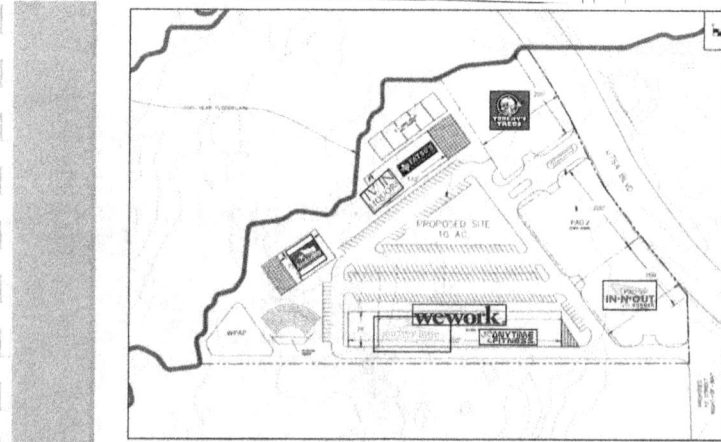

Attachment E: Initial Project Plan Sample

HAUSMAN PARK

Executive Summary

Vintage Real Estate, LLC is developing a 132,000 square foot retail shopping center, Hausman Park, on a 21 acre parcel at the corner of Hausman road and 1604 W. Hausman Park shopping Center is focused on creating an atmosphere, conducive to families and students, by uniquely providing a combination of "Family Focused" shopping center with a green space where the tenants, customers, and surrounding communities can enjoy Hausman Park in its entirety.

Hausman Road and 1604 is an area that is family based. Located in the northwest quadrant submarket of San Antonio, which to date is one of the largest growth areas of the area, accounting for at least 40% of San Antonio's total growth. Hausman Park is surrounded by

Vintage Real Estate, LLC
A Real Estate Development Company

multiple neighborhoods, schools, and continual expansion of San Antonio westward. Surrounding schools include Stinson Middle School, Brandeis High School, and the rapidly growing University of Texas at San Antonio, which is only a mile east of 1604, along with the 5 residential neighborhoods within the 3 mile radius area. Demographics show that the average income for this area is $81k per household. The traffic counts for Loop 1604 and Hausman are 76,000 and 11,000 vehicles per day respectively.

SITE LOCATION

PROJECT OVERLAY

Contracting such stores as Sprouts, Shoe Carnival, Hobby Lobby, Office Depot, along with the additions of Canes and Starbuck, Hausman Park will truly be family oriented.

A unique feature of Hausman Park will be The Creek at Hausman Park (The Creek). The Creek is a 6 acre green space filled with mature oak trees, a dry creek, park benches, and walking trails. This feature will be located at the east end of the property allowing the development to utilize all of the trees necessary to comply with the San Antonio Tree ordinance as well as take advantage of the 100 year flood plain restrictions. The north east corner of the property will be built up into a 1.5 acre square pad site to create a prime location at the corner of the intersection. The 1.5 acre pad site will then be sold to help provide additional funding to offset the landscaping costs of the 6 acre green pedestrian friendly area.

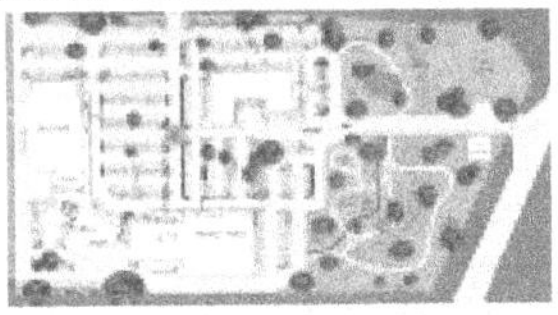

Vintage Real Estate, LLC
A Real Estate Development Company

Attachment F: Project; Cost, Operations and Profit

CLASS A OFFICE DEVELOPMENT

Development Cost Analysis

Land/Building Analysis

	Quantity/Sq. Ft.	Unit Cost	Total
Land Area			
Year One Ground Lease	197,850	4.54	
Net Land - Cost	3,122,668	$15.78	$3,122,668
Gross Building Area/$ per Buildable Ft.	71,318	$43.79	
Gross Rentable Areas/$ per Rentable Ft.	71,318	$43.79 0.00%	

Hard Cost

Building Shell/Sitework	71,318	$107.01	$7,631,470
GC Fee - Deferred Equity		$0.00	$0
GC Fee		$0.00	$0
Contingency		$5.35	$381,574
Sub-Total Hard Costs		$112.36	$8,013,044

Soft Cost

Inspections & Testing	0.4%	$0.45	$32,300
Geotechnical Report and Testing		$0.16	$11,308
Permits & Fees		$4.06	$289,263
Architectural		$5.13	$365,744
Civil Engineering		$1.23	$87,500
Code Consultant		$0.01	$1,000
Legal		$0.56	$40,000
Marketing		$5.08	$362,500
Property Taxes		$0.82	$58,500
Insurance		$0.16	$11,250
Office Supplies / Misc		$0.03	$2,000
Development Fee		$7.65	$545,709
Operating Expenses	0.40%	$2.95	$210,075
Contingency		$4.30	$306,690
Sub-Total Soft Cost		$32.58	$2,323,839
Total Hard & Soft Cost		$144.94	$10,336,883
Total Hard, Soft and Land Cost		$188.73	$13,459,561

Tenant Improvements, Commissions & Financing Cost

Leasing Commissions	6.00%		$897,730
Tenant Improvements (Base)		$46.94	$3,347,720
Sub-Total Development Cost		$249.66	$17,805,001
Financing Costs		$14.31	$1,020,603

Total Development Cost

Total Development Cost		$263.97	$18,825,604

Financing Analysis

Construction Debt

		Rate	Total
Construction Loan		75%	$14,119,203
Construction Finance Rate		4.00%	
Loan Fee (Construction)		0.5%	$70,596
Construction Loan Carry			$950,007
Total Construction Debt Costs			$1,020,603
Equity Contribution		25.00%	$4,706,401
Other - Equity Contribution		0.00%	$0
Total Contribution		25.00%	$4,706,401

Permanent Debt

Equity Required	$4,706,401.00	25%	
Permanent Loan	$14,119,203.01		
Rate	3.75%		
Amort.	25		
Payment	$871,095		
Debt Coverage Ratio	1.62 x's		

Rental Assumptions

	Square Feet	Rate	TI	Term
Anchor Tenant	33,000	$19.83	$55.00	10
Shadow Tenant	12,000	$22.00	$40.00	5
Speculative	22,752	$21.50	$0.00	0
Total	67,752	$20.78		
Percentage Leased	63%			

Stabilized NOI

	Total	SF / Year	YOC
Gross Revenue	$ 1,484,227	$ 20.81	7.88%
Less Vacancy Factor	$ (76,669)	$ (1.08)	
Effective Gross Income	$ 1,407,558	$ 19.74	7.48%
Operating Expense Reimbursement	$ 654,754	$ 9.18	
Ground Rent Reimbursement	$ -	$ -	
Total Revenues	$ 2,062,312	$ 28.92	
Operating Expenses			
Utilities	$ 99,845	$ 1.40	
CAM	$ 156,900	$ 2.20	
Property Tax	$ 320,931	$ 4.50	
Property Insurance	$ 17,830	$ 0.25	
Management Fee	$ 49,265	$ 0.69	
Accounting Fee	$ 9,985	$ 0.14	
Total Operating Expenses	$ 654,754	$ 9.18	
Ground Rent	$ -	$ -	
NET OPERATING INCOME	$ 1,407,558	$ 19.74	7.48%
Debt Service	$871,095		
Cash Flow	$ 536,463	$ 7.52	11.40%
Cash-on-Cash	11.40%		

Return Analysis

Hold Period (in Months)

	Start	Term
Pre-Construction	0	4
Construction	4	12
Rent Comment	16	18
Sell	34	

Exit Assumption

Methodology:	Direct Cap Rate
Vacancy Rate	5.0%
Cap Rate	7.25%
Cost of Sale	4.30%

Deal Returns

Dollars In	4,706,401
Dollars Out	6,787,946
Profit	2,081,545
Multiple	1.44 's
IRR	13.36%

Primary Equity

Preferred Return	7.0%		
25% to Primary Equity	Promote Over	7.0%	
* 10% to Secondary Equity			
	Equity	Clawback	Total
Dollars In	4,471,081		4,471,081
Dollars Out	6,236,950	158,699	6,395,649
Profit	1,765,870		1,924,568
Multiple	1.39 's		1.43 's
IRR	12.08%		13.04%

Developer Returns

	DEVELOPER	Clawback	Total
Dollars In	235,320		235,320
Dollars Out	445,196	(158,699)	286,498
Profit	209,876		51,178
Multiple	1.89 's		1.22 's
IRR	24.25%		#VALUE!

Secondary Equity

	Secondary Equity
Dollars In	0
Dollars Out	102,240
Profit	102,240

May 13, 2016   12:13 PM

KEY ASSUMPTIONS FOR THE DEVELOPMENT PROJECT:

1. To simplify the process this Guide will focus on developing an office or retail project. In this regard you should build no less than 10,000 sq. ft. of leasable space for an office or retail development.

2. This Guide is best utilized for new build projects not refurbishment of existing buildings. However the basic steps outlined in this Guide remains the same.

3. In choosing land site for a suburban oriented retail or office project assume the project site will need no less than one acre of land for every 10,000-15,000 square feet of leasable space.

4. To determine the purchase price of your land site find a land site listed with a commercial broker and use the greater of; negotiated purchase price with the seller, the average selling price or if no sale comps the average asking price for comparable land listed for sale. You can always use 100% of seller's asking price for the purchase price.

5. If you have out-parcels or pad sites assume they are sold or ground leased for a price and terms between 80-120% of average price and terms of comparable sales or ground leases for outparcel or pad sales in the area. For pro-forma purposes use the cash from any sale to pay down the construction loan.

6. The average lease rate per square foot for all tenants in the project should be between 80-120% of the average lease rate per square foot of the comparable projects.

7. The project should assume more than one tenant and you can assume up to 70% preleased space. We assume up to 70% preleased so the project is financeable. Assume all leases are no less than 3 years long and no more than 10. All leases should build in an inflation factor to be applied every year after the first full year at the rate of current CPI or 2 percent.

8. Use the average cost per gross square foot of the comps for estimating hard costs and you can use 10-15% of hard costs to estimate all soft costs.

9. All tenant leases should be modeled as triple net leases and you can assume a 5-10 percent vacancy factor. All leases should assume commissions at market rate or use 6%; 4% to tenant broker 2% to your broker.

10. The project should assume the construction lender will loan 70% of estimated total project cost. Therefore you need 30% of the project cost in equity investment. Use a current market interest rate, for the construction loan and the time it takes to "stabilize" the project should match up with the loan term.

11. The development project should contemplate no more than a 3-5 year project "hold period". The hold periods includes the estimated construction time including tenant build out and include time needed to stabilize and sell the project.

12. Assume any excess cash generated before sale is used to pay down construction loan and not distributed to the investors during the investment. Use a market "cumulative pref" or 8 percent or the equity investment and a 70/30 split of profit or "promote" between equity investor and the developer.

13. The development project should target a 15%, "ROI" deal return as a realistic minimum "go forward" threshold.

STEP BY STEP INDEX

WehrVentures

STEP BY STEP INDEX

STEP BY STEP INDEX

The Who, What, Where, Why and How Principles of
Developing CRE

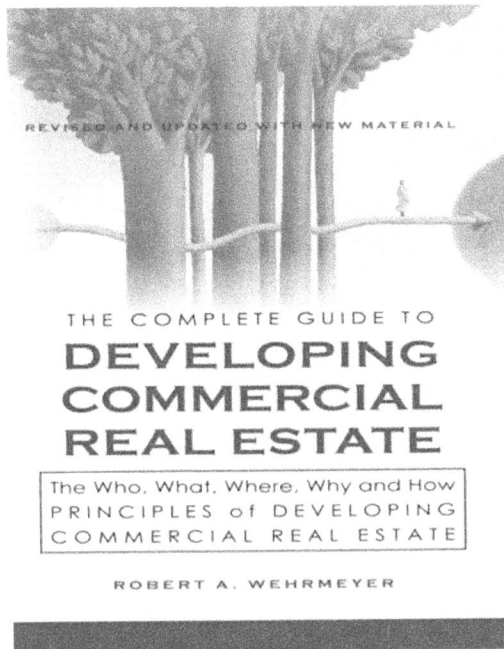

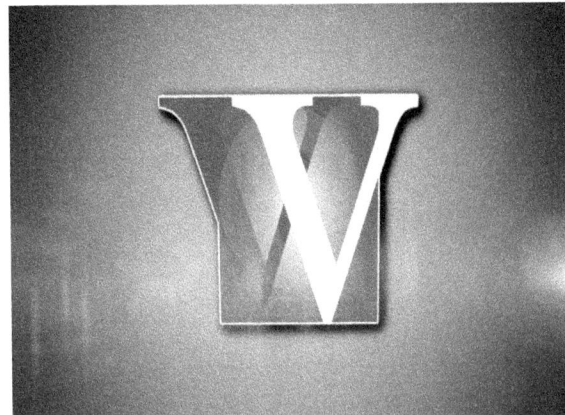

To access the documents referred to herein or order additional copies of this Guide, the

Principles Book or to access the author's,

Video Series please visit one of our web sites.

www.wehrventures.com or **www.developingcre.com**

The Who, What, Where, Why and How Principles of
Developing CRE

NOTES

NOTES

NOTES

www.ingramcontent.com/pod-product-compliance
Lightning Source LLC
Chambersburg PA
CBHW051229200326
41519CB00025B/7301